Motivation in the Workplace

Motivation in the Workplace

*How to Motivate Workers to Peak
Performance and Productivity*

Barbara Fielder

SkillPath Publications
Mission, Kansas

Editor: Kelly Scanlon

Cover and Book Design: Rod Hankins

ISBN: 1-878542-83-4

Library of Congress Catalog Card Number: 96-68884

10   9   8   7   6   5   4   02   03   04   05

Printed in the United States of America

Contents

Preface

What motivates workers has long puzzled supervisors and managers. When I began delivering training seminars and workshops more than a decade ago, managers and supervisors showed a special interest in the motivation segment of the program. And they still do today. These managers, like you, are seeking the formula for a motivational work environment and motivated employees.

This book is the result of years of informal research based on a simple question I've asked managers and supervisors in hundreds of workshops and seminars: What are you doing now to create a work environment where employees can be motivated out of desire rather than fear? Throughout the years, I've received dozens of practical ideas and suggestions from participants. More important, over the years, my seminar participants have reinforced the responses of managers and supervisors I'd spoken to years before—tried-and-true approaches that continue to generate results over time. This book focuses on those time-tested ideas. In the following pages, you will find easy-to-implement approaches and steps you can take every day to create a motivational work environment in your organization. As you read, consider whether you and your organization are currently using these approaches. If you are, are you using them successfully? If you're not using them, which ones lend themselves to practical implementation within your particular work environment?

The Benefits of a Motivated Workplace

"Everything that enlarges the sphere of human powers, that shows man he can do what he thought he could do, is valuable."

—Samuel Johnson

Motivation is widely acclaimed as a key to an empowered, self-directed, and *productive* work environment. As a manager, you can motivate employees through your own example as well as by implementing specific techniques that foster openness, a willing attitude, dedication, and mutual understanding among employees and between employees and management.

The overall benefits are twofold:

1. Workers feel personally satisfied and fulfilled.

2. The organization meets its goals.

2

You'll learn about some of these specific techniques in detail in Chapter 2. For now, consider just a few of the benefits—to the organization, to workers, and to you—of a motivational work climate:

- Workers achieve or exceed performance expectations.
- Workers cooperate with one another.
- Co-workers treat each other with respect.
- A team spirit exists.
- Workers are absent less often.
- Optimism replaces pessimism.
- Workers value customers rather than consider them a nuisance.
- Workers meet deadlines.
- Workers achieve or exceed quality performance levels.
- There is a noticeable improvement in worker/supervisor relationships.
- Communication is enhanced.

As you can see, the list of advantages of a highly motivated workforce goes on and on. But the one benefit every manager or supervisor consistently views as a plus is that the work employees perform meets expectations. This improvement in performance results largely from cooperation and teamwork, two other benefits of a motivated workplace.

As you read further, you'll learn about these benefits in greater detail and what you can do to nurture motivation in the people you manage. Consider whether your organization is currently enjoying these benefits, and focus on any areas where you could specifically improve.

Chapter One

Who's Motivated— and Why

(Your choice)

The good news is that everyone is motivated. The bad news is that you can't *personally* motivate anyone, whether you're a manager, a friend, a spouse, or a parent. People do things for their own reasons—not yours. Motivation comes from *within* each person.

So how can you, as a manager, create a motivated work environment when you can't personally motivate each of your employees?

To begin to answer that question, just think about your own situation. Why do you comply with the boss's requests? Do you do what's asked because you believe there's a benefit to you? Does compliance mean a future with the organization? a job promotion? better job opportunities? higher pay? a better relationship with your supervisor? positive comments from colleagues? Or, do you comply because you fear losing your job, being demoted, or having to do unpleasant jobs if you don't? Quite simply, are you motivated by desire or by fear?

Fear As a Motivator?

Managers have long used fear as a basic motivator. The obvious problem with using fear as a "motivator" is that workers eventually begin to loathe the object of their fear—the manager—and productivity levels begin to deteriorate rather than to increase. In the long run, workers who are afraid of the negative consequences a manager heaps upon them are likely to hate the supervisor and do little, if anything, to follow the supervisor's directions. In his book *Bringing Out the Best in People,* Aubrey C. Daniels[1] asserts that using fear to start people on the road toward better behavior may work initially, but a wise manager will positively reinforce each improvement.

Certainly, fear can't be considered a long-term motivator. Let's look then at several key theories of motivation that managers have studied over the last several decades.

"Only positive consequences encourage good future performance."

—Kenneth H. Blanchard and Robert Lorber in *Putting the One Minute Manager to Work*

---

[1]Aubrey C. Daniels, *Bringing Out the Best in People* (New York: McGraw-Hill, 1994).

Maslow's Hierarchy of Needs

Maslow's[2] theory of motivation suggests that each of us has individual needs and that we take action to satisfy those needs. Whichever need is strongest at any given time motivates us to take action to meet that need.

According to Maslow, a need motivates us as long as it *is not* satisfied. Once the need is satisfied, it no longer motivates us— yet we remain motivated. Maslow suggested that when your

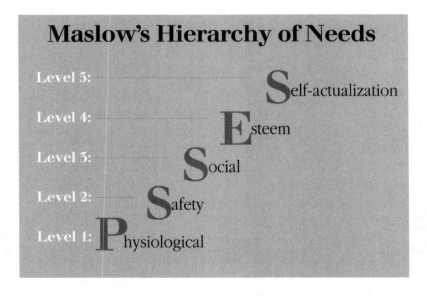

"No passion so effectually robs the mind of all its power of acting and reasoning as fear."

—Edmund Burke

---

[2]Abraham H. Maslow, *Motivation and Personality* (New York: Harper & Row, 1954).

need at any one level is satisfied, the needs of the next level become most critical and so on, creating an ongoing cycle of motivation. He grouped human needs in a hierarchy, according to their level of importance.

The first level covers the basic human needs: food, clothing, and shelter. Once these needs are met, the needs of the next level, safety and security, become the important motivators. This level not only suggests that we are motivated to remove physical dangers from our lives, but also that we need to *perceive* that we are free from danger and are therefore safe.

Several years ago Doreen, a woman in her mid-twenties, interviewed for an entry-level position in a large organization. She had *little* experience, yet a *big* need. She was a single working parent. She expressed that any job would do, any job that would help her provide food, shelter, and clothing for her child. These needs weren't for her welfare but for someone she loved and cared for deeply. In her interview, Doreen emphasized she would bring a sense of dedication to her job, even though she was light on skills. The company offered Doreen the job, and she jumped at the opportunity. Not only did she find it possible to feed, clothe, and shelter her child with her paycheck, she was able to meet the second need: She was able to move to a different neighborhood to ensure her child's safety. Once Doreen met these physiological, safety, and security needs, they were no longer her primary motivators. She discovered the needs of the third level of Maslow's hierarchy.

The third motivator in the hierarchy is associated with the need to belong and to experience closeness and group affiliation. Group affiliation also implies that we need approval and acceptance from the group.

Doreen discovered that once she was able to fulfill the needs of the first two levels, belonging, closeness, and group affiliation became important to her. She joined the company's bowling league. Doreen and her child spent several hours each week having fun and experiencing group interaction and affiliation with other employees.

The next need level is esteem; that is, recognition as being outstanding in some way that makes us feel good about ourselves. Doreen realized that the recognition of her colleagues and her bowling league friends was important to her. She did her best during the game. More important, she strived for excellent performance on the job. She enjoyed the recognition of her peers and supervisor as she improved her job skills and performance levels.

The highest level of needs is self-actualization. Often difficult to describe, this level is strongly related to your perception of life, ideas, and what you want out of it, of your values and what you strive for.

In Doreen's case, going back to school to increase her skill level and increase her opportunity for promotion was the highest level of need. Not only did this goal help her meet her personal maximum potential, she believed that with a higher level of education and increased skill level, she would be able to perform her job and improve her opportunities for promotion. She believed that, ultimately, she would be able to provide a strong, secure, and happy life for herself and her child.

As you can see, there are many opportunities to apply Maslow's theory on the job. One of the challenges, of course, is trying to understand where each worker is in the hierarchy. A worker who is at the physiological level won't be motivated by the same things as someone who's progressed to the self-actualization level. Part of your job as a supervisor is building a relationship with those you supervise so you know their current individual needs and therefore what motivates them. The accompanying table provides an overview of how you as a manager or supervisor might use Maslow's theory in the workplace. Chapters 2 and 3 will discuss some of these suggestions in more detail.

"The only way I can get you to do anything is by giving you what you want."

—Dale Carnegie

Maslow's Needs Hierarchy Applied on the Job

Level 1—Physiological: The need for food, clothing, shelter, rest, health
- Adequate rest and meal breaks
- Wages and benefits sufficient to provide basic needs

Level 2—Safety and security: The need to feel safe
- Opportunities for training so workers will feel secure about job skills
- Adherence to health and safety codes
- Recognition for long-term service to company

Level 3—Social: The need to belong
- Work in teams or units
- Department or company social events (picnics, potlucks, milestone celebrations)
- Company sporting events

Level 4—Esteem: The need to be recognized for outstanding work or other accomplishments
- Employee recognition and reward systems
- Opportunities to train or teach others

Level 5—Self-actualization: The need to find meaning
- Opportunity to do challenging work
- Work autonomously
- Job rotation
- Training
- Provisions for extended medical or emergency leave

12

Herzberg's "Job Satisfiers"

Yet another motivational theory advanced in the 1950s is that of psychologist Frederick Herzberg.[3] Herzberg asserted that certain factors contribute to workers' job satisfaction and can therefore be considered workplace motivators. Applying Herzberg's theory, then, the job of a manager or supervisor trying to create a motivating workplace environment is to identify those workplace factors that contribute to job satisfaction. Herzberg himself identified some of these during his research:

- Achievement and advancement
- Recognition
- Challenging work and responsibility

He found that each of these seemed to motivate workers to perform better. On the other hand, he also identified potential "dissatisfiers," which he termed "hygiene" factors:

- Company policies and procedures
- Wages and benefits
- Relationships with co-workers and supervisors
- General working conditions

It's important to note that Herzberg's research led him to believe that although these "hygiene" factors can definitely have a demotivating effect, they cannot have a *long-term motivating* effect. Why? Quite simply, these factors don't allow for personal growth and achievement (recall Maslow's top two levels of needs: esteem and self-actualization).

---

[3]Frederick Herzberg et al. *The Motivation to Work* (New York: Wiley, 1959).

In practical terms, what this theory means to you as a supervisor trying to create a motivated, productive work environment is that you must provide opportunities for growth and achievement and then recognize those achievements in a timely fashion. Describe to workers exactly what they achieved and the impact the achievement had on the overall outcome of the project. When you recognize employees, you provide positive direction for continued successful performance. In Chapter 2, you will read about ways to provide challenging work and suggestions for setting up reward and recognition systems.

Understanding Your Supervisory Style

You have seen how employees can be motivated by need and by desire for growth and achievement. One often-overlooked factor when it comes to motivating employees is supervisory style. Your own beliefs about employees influences your supervisory style, which in turn has a major impact on their level of motivation.

Douglas McGregor[4], a professor of industrial management at M.I.T., suggests in his Theory X and Theory Y concepts that it may be more helpful to managers to understand their management style and personal beliefs about their employees rather than individual employee motivators.

A manager who supports the Theory X idea assumes that employees lack ambition, find their work distasteful, have little or no desire to take on responsibility, want to be directed in the

---

[4]Douglas McGregor, *The Human Side of Enterprise* (New York: McGraw-Hill, 1960).

performance of their duties, and don't want to contribute to developing creative solutions to workplace problems. Adherents of Theory X believe that the worker's total focus is on personal safety and job security and, therefore, that the key motivators are money, benefits, and fear. A Theory X manager's approach to working with employees is to give them a "short leash," to oversupervise. In other words, such managers believe that workers will perform their job duties only if told precisely what to do and how to do it and then only if watched over.

In contrast to Theory X, Theory Y assumes that workers are reliable, that they don't shirk job duties, that they can and do contribute to creative problem solving, and that good work can be performed, even in a self-directed fashion. In organizations where managers apply Theory Y, workers are given greater levels of responsibility and are provided with plenty of information, including the "whys" that are necessary to getting the job done. Employees' ideas and decisions are sought out to improve job performance. According to Theory Y, the manager is a leader who paves the way for employees to become successful. Gathering employee ideas and involving them in decision-making would definitely be a part of this approach.

"Nothing creates more self-respect among employees than being included in the process of making decisions."

—Judith Bardwick in *The Plateauing Trap*

Obviously, adherents of Theory X take a much more autocratic approach to supervising. They use the "carrot-and-stick" method of rewarding employees who perform well and punishing those who perform below par. Employees working under such managers may never have an opportunity at work to fulfill the need levels at the top of Maslow's hierarchy. Similarly, Theory X managers lean towards satisfying the potential "dissastisfiers" Herzberg identified rather than focusing on providing job-related satisfiers such as challenging work, achievement, and recognition.

Still, some Theory Y supervisors are disappointed with the productivity of the employees they manage. Some employees, especially those accustomed to working for Theory X supervisors, have trouble adjusting to the looser controls, participation, and independence a Theory Y manager may encourage. As a result, productivity may actually plummet because of what employees perceive as a lack of direction.

A rather recent "middle" ground many managers have adopted is called Theory Z, which suggests a more flexible approach appropriate for the situation and the employee involved. Of course, Theory Z requires supervisors to know the project circumstances and individual employees well in order to adapt their supervisory style to each situation and employee. A rather exaggerated example that highlights Theory Z in action is that if you're a predominately Theory Y style of manager but are in a room filled with smoke and the fire alarm is wailing, you won't consult workers to gain consensus on exit procedures. You'll take charge and direct a speedy, safe, and secure exit of the facility.

16

Now that you have the theoretical basis for what motivates workers, you'll learn in Chapter 2 some practical suggestions for applying these theories.

Chapter Two

Creating a Motivated Workplace

What "Activates" Workplace Motivation?

Although motivation must come from within each person, as a manager, you can make a significant contribution to creating a positive work environment. But it has to be an ongoing effort. Research indicates that it takes about ten to twenty-one repetitions to develop a new habit. And when you get in the habit of activating workplace motivation, two things will happen. First, your employees will know exactly what behaviors are important for them to demonstrate on the job and what level of performance you expect. Second, you will enhance communication and foster a motivating environment.

You can take your first step in creating a highly motivated work environment by implementing any—or all—of the ideas and strategies in this chapter. They were generated by seminar participants during small group discussions focusing on the actions leaders can take to activate positive behaviors in workers.

Acknowledge Employees

Recognition...feedback...praise...thank you...appreciation— these are all ways you can acknowledge workers and their performance. Research indicates that the number one thing employees want is recognition. Recognition can take the form of verbal praise, a thoughtful note, positive feedback during a performance appraisal, a public announcement (at a meeting, in the company newsletter, or on the department bulletin board) that shares the accomplishment with other employees, managers, and company executives.

"Good words are worth much, and cost little."

—George Herbert, English clergyman

No More Excuses

But if acknowledging workers plays such an important role in worker motivation, why are managers often so stingy in passing out the praise? Here are a few of the common reasons:

- I get too busy.
- I just seem to forget in the press of day-to-day business.
- By the time I get around to doing something about a good performance, too much time has passed and then it's too late.

Sound familiar? If you're guilty of making any of these excuses, consider the old adage "you pay now or you pay later." If you fail to give recognition now, you'll likely pay later—in terms of low morale, absenteeism, and employee turnover. Don't risk the possibility of losing terrific employees. Apply the SSPT formula to make employee praise and recognition a regular—and important—part of your management routine.

"Celebrate what you want to see more of."

—Tom Peters in *Thriving on Chaos*

Specific. Make sure the employee has no doubt about what actions or behavior you're recognizing.

Sincere. Use a warm tone of voice, smile, and make eye contact. The employee must believe that you mean what you say.

Personalized. Use the employee's name often.

Timely. Recognize an event, performance, or behavior as closely as possible to the date it occurred. Waiting for the performance review diminishes the effect of the feedback and does nothing to ensure that the employee will continue the desired behaviors.

Another way to remind yourself to make employee praise and recognition a part of your routine is to practice the "ten-coin" technique. Place ten coins of any denomination in your right pocket. The ten coins jingling in your pocket will remind you to acknowledge employees. Each time you give an employee a positive comment, praise, or recognition, remove a coin from your right pocket and place it in your left pocket. As your day progresses, you can reach into your left pocket, take out the loose change, and quickly find out how many times you've recognized employees that particular day.

The idea is to make positive feedback a regular part of your communication with employees. Too often employees say, "The only time I hear from my supervisor is when things are really messed up."

Forms of Acknowledgment

So what are some of the ways you can acknowledge employees? You're probably familiar with the traditional awards, banquets, gold watches, clocks, and bonuses. All of these can be effective and do have their place.

Many forward-thinking organizations, however, have begun to develop more creative forms of employee acknowledgment. These nontraditional and often non-money forms of recognition are being used successfully in many companies:

- Employee of the month
- Employee financial, retirement, or savings consultations, paid for by the company
- Work-at-home options
- Health and fitness seminars and programs
- Casual dress days
- Department pizza parties or potluck lunches
- Company-paid training programs and seminars
- Dinner gift certificates at local restaurants
- Paid time off for charitable activities
- Flex-time
- Employee-of-the-week/month parking space

Which types of rewards would work best in your organization? Consider the following:

- *Your organization's corporate culture.* Is it more traditional? Does the "unique" send chills down the CEO's spine? Or, does your organization embrace change and exhibit a willingness to try new ideas?

- *Your organization's image.* Does your organization project a sleek, corporate image, or is it more casual?

- *The types of behaviors you want to reward.* You may want to consider a multi-tiered reward system that acknowledges more profound accomplishments and achievements with greater rewards.

- *The amount of time your department or organization can give to an employee on-the-job recognition event.* The reward system must be practical. If you announce a system you can't follow up on, the effect will be lower morale rather than motivated workers.

Empower Employees

To "empower" means "to allow or enable." Successful leaders conduct themselves in such a way that employees feel good about working with them. How do they do this? By enabling and allowing employees to succeed. Empowered employees feel ownership of their work, a critical element to creating a motivated workplace. The ten steps that follow are necessary to cultivating empowered employees.

1. *Delegate meaningful jobs, not just the "junk" stuff you don't want to do.* Workers don't want to perform trivial tasks on a regular basis any more than you do. If the tasks are truly unimportant, maybe they should be deleted altogether. If they are necessary, consider setting up a rotating schedule so workers can take turns performing the task.

2. *"Let go" once you delegate (supervisors have a tendency to oversupervise).* If you delegate a task, make sure the person you give it to has the skills, the instructions, and the resources necessary to carry it out. If you don't have confidence in the person's ability to do a satisfactory job, you shouldn't give the task to that person to begin with.

3. *Show you trust your employees by accepting their ideas and suggestions.* Seek out employees' ideas on a regular basis. Employees feel ownership of a process or a task when they've had input into it.

4. ***Whenever possible, provide opportunities for employees to work in self-managed or self-directed work teams.*** Allow these teams freedom to determine the best course of action for meeting agreed-upon goals and objectives. Employees will see firsthand the results of their decisions and feel the pride of group achievement.

5. ***Give credit where credit is due.*** A sure way to earn distrust from employees and squelch their enthusiasm is to take credit for their good ideas and performances.

6. ***Create opportunities to showcase your employees.*** "Billboard" employees to your own supervisors and to others in upper management as well as to those outside your department or division.

Some managers erroneously think that if they give workers credit, upper management will question the manager's own performance. But managers who fall into the trap of competing with the employees they supervise usually stall their own careers. Consider this: If you're a manager, where do you think you're going if there is no one to fill *your* shoes? Have you ever had a conversation with a boss about your future? Have you ever been disappointed when he or she said, "You're a great asset to the company, but I don't foresee a move for you in the near future."

"Setting and communicating the right expectations is the most important tool a manager has for imparting that elusive drive to the people he supervises."

—Andrew S. Grove in *One-on-One With Andy Grove*

Naturally, your response would have been, "Why?"

And your boss's response probably went something like this: "I can't afford to let you go because my boss believes there's no one to take your place."

What happened? There was a very talented and gifted person who could easily have performed your job, yet this person was the best-kept secret in the department. In this situation, it may have become painfully clear that it's important to billboard the workers you supervise.

7. ***Add interest and challenge to workers' day-to-day routines by implementing job rotation.*** Job rotation simply involves placing employees into jobs of equal value that they may have expressed an interest in or that you expect, based on their skill strengths, they may do well in. Some organizations, such as Duke Power, encourage employees to initiate job rotation through a formal process, thereby increasing job skill levels as well as motivation.

For example, in 1993, Duke Power initiated a job swap program for its 17,600-member workforce. This program allows employees who are dissatisfied with their job for any reason to post it on an electronic bulletin board and actively seek out other employees who may be interested in trading jobs. Before the "swap" can take place, each employee's supervisor must give approval.

This interesting approach has merit. For one, it provides the organization with a pool of employees who can perform a variety of jobs with little training. And because the employees come from within the organization, they are already familiar with the organization and the corporate culture. It's a win-win situation. The organization sees an increase in employee morale and motivation, but with no recruitment cost.

Furthermore, because this unique approach to job rotation is employee-initiated, the employee anxiety normally associated with making a job change is minimal.

Keep in mind, however, that although a job rotation program will be a welcome change for some employees, others will view it with trepidation. It is important that you be ready to answer employees' questions as you prepare them for job rotation. Here are some points you may wish to consider before implementing such a program:

- The job duties to be performed
- The performance expectations or goals
- The reason the employee was selected (excellent performance, attendance record, a willingness to learn, an optimistic attitude, leadership abilities, etc.)
- Who the employee will turn to for information and advice
- The duration of the new assignment, including beginning and ending dates
- How performance will be evaluated

Often job rotation is not possible due to the limited number of job opportunities within the company or because of time constraints. In these instances, it is still possible to challenge employees with a variety of job responsibilities. The solution is to use teams whenever possible. As a team member, each employee becomes involved in decision making, problem solving, and all phases of a project. Teams also encourage employees to take calculated risks to experience group achievement.

8. ***Provide employees with responsibility and authority to successfully accomplish assignments.*** Today, progressive companies utilize the skills and talents of their employees by assigning them to cross-functional or self-directed work teams. Employees not only perform their own specific job functions but have a team identity as well. Team members are responsible and accountable to the team for achieving its goal, implementing processes, and sharing the recognition for its results.

9. ***Provide assistance to employees without taking away their responsibility to complete the job.*** Clearly define your role and avoid the temptation to do the job yourself when employees find themselves in hot water.

Some supervisors have a lingering doubt about turning over jobs or tasks without reserving some personal control. This style of management is frequently referred to as *micromanagement.* If you hang on to the reins, you'll choke out the creativity that employees can bring (willingly) to the job. There's no such thing as partial trust. If you're in doubt about how far you can delegate and trust the employee to do the job, do it incrementally.

Someone wisely said "inch by inch it's a cinch; yard by yard it's hard." Let employees go it on their own and face those gut-wrenching challenges. Those who succeed will feel the dizzying, delirious satisfaction of accomplishment and be motivated to tackle new projects

10. ***Find ways to foster employee self-esteem and self-confidence.*** Although important, managers and supervisors must do more than give praise and provide meaningful work. To empower employees, supervisors must continually build employee self-esteem. Here are several suggestions for doing so:

- Ask for help in solving problems.

- Practice MBWA—Management By Walking Around, a phrase and philosophy made popular by Mr. Hewlett and Mr. Packard, co-founders of Hewlett-Packard. Routinely walk through the office or the shop floor so employees know you're available.

- Provide a suggestion box or develop other programs to elicit ideas and suggestions for work or quality improvement. Make sure everyone's ideas are noted, and keep employees informed about the status of their suggestions. If you make the mistake of implementing a suggestion program and fail to follow up on ideas, employees will soon realize that management is only making a pretense of being interested in their suggestions.

- Implement a quality circle program that allows employees to suggest ways for continuous improvement in products and services.

- Create a team environment that allows employees to attain greater levels of success through mutual goal setting, achievement, and recognition.

Managers and supervisors must show employees their own personal level of commitment to the ideas that are generated and take employee creativity seriously. Doing so sends employees a strong message that it's okay to come up with some off-the-wall ideas without the fear of a rebuff.

Mistakes Are Okay

Not long ago, a story circulated about a young man who made a mistake that had a serious and substantial financial impact on his company. He feared that he would be fired for making this error, so he whipped up his letter of resignation and touched up his resumé for a hasty job search. The big boss was out of town, so the young man left the letter of resignation on the boss's desk and waited for him to return. When the boss arrived back at the office, he summoned the young man at once. The young man was ready to take his licks, but then a surprising thing happened. The boss refused to accept the resignation. The boss told him that the company had just invested a substantial amount of money in his *on-the-job* training and he was not

> "Go ahead and fail... but fail with wit, fail with grace, fail with style. A mediocre failure is as insufferable as a mediocre success. Embrace failure, seek it out, learn to love it."
>
> —Tom Peters

going anywhere. He was going to stay. The moral of this story, as you might guess, is that you must allow employees to make mistakes without the fear of losing their jobs.

Certainly, you will create boundaries and advise employees who are learning their jobs. But a good manager recognizes that employees will only get better and grow in their jobs by squarely facing the challenges associated with making tough decisions and living with the consequences. Living with the tried and true will certainly limit mistakes, but it will limit you to mediocrity.

Make Having Fun a Routine

Many organizations have discovered the value of instilling a sense of humor and fun in the workplace. In fact, in a recent survey, executives indicated that a sense of humor is extremely valuable in maintaining a motivated work environment. Employees with a sense of humor are viewed as:

- Good communicators.
- Team players.
- Stress reducers.

When employees have fun at work, they have a greater interest in their jobs and come together for reasons other than the day-to-day work routine. You may recall that Maslow considered social interaction to be a primary motivator.

Why not provide the opportunity for "fun" in your organization? Here are a few ideas to consider:

- Publish a short column in the company newsletter that features fun stories, silly workplace anecdotes, or personal experiences.

- Keep a camera handy to take pictures of department events and then post them on the bulletin board with a funny caption.

- Have an employee talent show. One hospital stages an annual "lip sync" show. Each department's employees sing and perform to their favorite recording artist's song. The employees dress in costumes and have a great time. A panel of judges selects the best performance, but all participants receive a prize. The grand prize winners receive a special gift.

- Organize a company baseball, bowling, or volleyball team. Write up game results in the company newsletter. Have an awards ceremony to present trophies or gag gifts to all event participants. You'll be amazed at the camaraderie sports teams can create—and at how much of that team spirit carries over to work.

Earn Trust

Time and time again, employees identify trust as necessary for creating a motivating workplace environment. Trust employees to do the job, to behave responsibly, to follow the path to goal achievement, and to work autonomously. You'll recall that this is the leadership style described in McGregor's Theory Y.

> *"The only way to make a man trustworthy is to trust him."*
>
> —Henry Stimson, U.S. Secretary of War during World War II

Be a Role Model

Leadership entails some awesome responsibilities. One of these is modeling the kinds of behaviors you expect of workers. Your employees will follow your lead, and you'll see immediate results.

Ask yourself:

1. Do I keep myself motivated? Do I keep my enthusiasm and optimism high by setting realistic goals and celebrating my successes?

2. Do I learn from my mistakes and take alternative steps so I'll succeed in the future?

3. Do I teach by example?

4. Am I a positive role model to colleagues, family, and friends?

Communicate, Communicate, Communicate

There's no way to overstress the importance of communication in creating a motivated work environment. It's one of the most powerful tools you have at your disposal. When your employees are informed and know "the big picture," they understand the purpose and rationale behind their tasks and can perform their jobs better.

There are several keys to creating effective two-way communication. Here are several of them:

- Make sure that your words, tone, and body language are congruent.

- Practice active listening.

- Make yourself available to employees.

- Be receptive to employee feedback.

The Importance of Congruency

Many people erroneously believe that their words are the most important vehicle for getting their message across. Actually, three elements are involved in all communications:

1. Words

2. Tone

3. Body language

People tend to believe what they see. To deliver a believable message to others, your body language must be congruent with your words and with the tone of voice you use to deliver the message.

"Accurate information is a key part of motivation."

—Mary Ann Allison and Eric Allison in *Managing Up, Managing Down*

Your body language cues your listener to your level of knowledge about the subject, your level of interest, and your level of cooperation. In addition, your body language reveals whether you are being honest with your listener.

Remember, your message is credible only when your body language, tone, and words are congruent.

Be an Active Listener

Has anyone ever told you that you weren't listening? Have you ever asked others to repeat themselves, because your mind had wandered? Have you ever taken a mental "leave of absence" while someone was speaking? Have you ever been embarrassed because you gave the wrong answer to a question when you weren't listening? Has anyone ever asked you whether you're paying attention? If you answered "yes" to any of these questions, then you have some room to grow as an effective listener.

Listening is probably one of the most difficult communication skills to master, but the most essential if you want to convey the message that you're interested in what employees are saying. Managers who don't listen are essentially telling employees they're not receptive to feedback or suggestions. It's a sure-fire way to quickly discourage even the most motivated workers from sharing their ideas.

Here are eleven active listening techniques you'll need to master to ensure that you're really listening:

1. ***Stop talking.*** There's absolutely no way you can listen when you're talking.

2. ***Put the sender at ease.*** Help your sender feel free to talk.

3. ***Show that you want to listen.*** Make eye contact and look and act interested in the sender. When you're listening, don't read your mail, take telephone calls, or watch other people.

4. ***Remove distractions.*** Don't doodle, tap, shuffle papers, click your mechanical pencil or pen, or make high-tech widgets with your paper clips.

5. ***Be empathetic.*** This means to put yourself in the sender's place so you can understand his or her point of view. Try to look at the issue from a point of agreement rather than disagreement.

6. ***Be patient.*** Give yourself plenty of time to listen. Don't rush the conversation. Don't interrupt or finish your sender's sentences. Avoid walking away or heading for the door.

7. ***Hold your temper.*** Your emotions can influence how you hear and emphasize your sender's words. If you're an angry listener, you can derive the wrong meaning from your sender's words.

8. Lighten up on your criticism and avoid being argumentative. Criticism and argumentative tones can quickly put the sender on the defensive. The sender may "clam up" or, just the opposite, "get in your face." Avoid arguing. Even if you win, you ultimately lose.

9. Ask questions. If the sender is a person of few words and hasn't made the message clear to you, ask open-ended questions. But when your sender is long-winded and you want a "yes" or "no" response, ask a closed-ended question.

10. Paraphrase. Send back to your sender the message you heard, in your own words. This technique reinforces the listening effort. It allows the sender to hear the message as you received it and it gives you additional time to digest the information and develop your response.

11. Stop talking. This was the first suggestion to active listening and it's also the last. You just can't do a good job of listening while you're talking.

Be Available

Two-way communication can't take place if you're always behind a closed door. Let your employees know you're available to answer questions, hear ideas, or help with problems, if only for a specified period of time each day. Remember the MBWA technique discussed previously. It's a simple way to make yourself accessible to employees as well as an excellent way to acquire firsthand knowledge of the day-to-day operations of your department or work unit.

Encourage Feedback

Any two-way communication involves feedback. You've already learned how to encourage feedback from employees by using active listening skills and by keeping employees informed about the status of their ideas and suggestions. Now, here are some tips for giving feedback to employees:

1. Find a quiet place where you can give your undivided attention to your employee.

2. Make eye contact.

3. Make sure your facial expression and tone of voice convey the same message as your words. Stay attentive when the employee speaks.

4. Use the employee's name periodically during the conversation.

5. Follow-up with a handshake and a summary of the points you made, to ensure clarification and understanding.

Motivation Checkup

Place a check mark in the appropriate column to quickly rate yourself on the frequency with which you activate these motivators in your workplace.

	Almost always	Sometimes	Rarely
1. Give recognition	☑	☐	☐
2. Delegate meaningful work	☐	☑	☐
3. Provide opportunities for self-management	☐	☑	☐
4. Give credit when due	☑	☐	☐
5. Showcase employees	☐	☑	☐
6. Provide opportunities for job rotation	☐	☑	☐
7. Solicit employee ideas and suggestions	☑	☐	☐
8. Ensure workers have authority and resources to accomplish job tasks and assignments	☑	☐	☐
9. Practice MBWA	☑	☐	☐
10. Provide opportunities to work in teams when possible	☑	☐	☐

11. Tolerate mistakes as part of the learning process ☑ ☐ ☐

12. Encourage activities that make work fun and upbeat ☐ ☑ ☐

13. Act as a role model ☑ ☐ ☐

14. Show employees that you trust them and, likewise, that they can trust you ☑ ☐ ☐

15. Listen actively ☑ ☐ ☐

16. Encourage employee feedback ☑ ☐ ☐

18. Provide regular and ongoing feedback ☐ ☑ ☐

19. Communicate credibly ☑ ☐ ☐

How did you fare? Obviously, depending on the type of work you do and the number of employees you manage, you can't implement each of the motivators on the list on a daily basis. However, some of the items listed are possible in any situation (e.g., active listening, providing feedback). Choose one or two actions that you aren't currently practicing and try to make it part of the regular routine. Make these actions part of the goals you set when you sketch out your Motivation Action Plan in Chapter 4.

Chapter Three

Combating Managerial Actions That Lead to Workplace "De-Motivation"

As you discovered in chapters 1 and 2, the choices you make everyday influence the motivational climate of your company. Obviously, you want to implement in your workplace as many of the suggestions from Chapter 2 as possible. Likewise, you'll want to know which actions to avoid—and how to do so. This chapter takes a look at several "de-motivating" actions that many managers routinely practice.

Survey results published in the April 1994 issue of *Personnel Journal* noted that 150 executives from the nation's 1,000 largest companies identified the following as ways in which managers damage employee's morale:

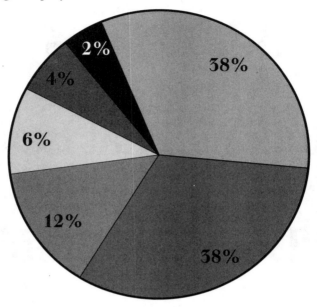

Criticizing in front of others	38%
Being dishonest	38%
Taking credit for others' work	12%
Being inaccessible	6%
Showing favoritism	4%
Don't know	2%

Source: Accountemps

In addition to the negative actions in the previous survey results, attendees at over five hundred leadership seminars indicated that managers and other organizational leaders often make the following crucial mistakes, which lead to low morale and workplace de-motivation:

- Delegating without giving authority, or delegating to the wrong person
- Communicating poorly or failing to communicate at all
- Failing to train employees for job responsibilities
- Exhibiting wishy-washy behavior
- Failing to emphasize teamwork
- Giving the impression that you're concerned only about your own well-being
- Displaying poor personal work habits such as disorganization and procrastination
- Tolerating poor performance
- Oversupervising
- Imposing impossible workloads
- Focusing only on negatives

Let's examine each of these in turn.

Criticizing in Front of Others

If you must discipline an employee, do so *privately*. When you criticize publicly, you risk embarrassing the employee in front of peers. You may actually escalate the situation because the employee may counter his or her embarrassment by reacting defensively to your message.

In addition, when you make a habit of criticizing workers in front of their peers, you create an environment in which employees are afraid to make mistakes, which are a normal and vital part of the learning process.

Being Dishonest

Trust is the foundation of every strong supervisor-employee relationship. A supervisor who is dishonest breeds distrust. Employees won't believe what they're told and won't respect a supervisor who isn't straightforward. Be upfront with your employees about what's going on in the organization. If you're not at liberty to discuss a situation, say so rather than making something up to pacify the worker who asked.

Another form of dishonesty is having a set of standards for you and one for workers. Don't use your rank as supervisor as a cover for bending company policies to your benefit but expect workers to comply.

Taking Credit for Others' Work

As you learned in Chapter 2, taking credit for employees' accomplishments results in two things. First, employees will resent you and won't see the value in doing their best if they know you're always going to take the credit. Further, they won't be around to support you when the going gets rough.

Second, if you always take the credit rather than letting the spotlight shine on those who deserve it, you can ruin your own chances for promotion. Upper management will think you're so good in your current position that no one can replace you. In the long run, you risk demotivating employees and ruining your own chances of advancement when you steal others' glory.

Being Inaccessible

One of the most important contributions you can make to creating a motivational work environment is to acknowledge your employees on a regular basis. One way to do this is to make yourself available to employees. Regularly activate "management by walking around" (MBWA). When you get out of your office and go out to the work area, you give employees who otherwise may not walk into your office the opportunity to approach you. The three Bs to your success here are:

1. **BE** visible.

2. **BE** informative.

3. **BE** available.

Take time from your day—in fact schedule a regular part of your day—to MBWA. Supervisors who are inaccessible send the message that what employees do and what they need don't matter.

Showing Favoritism

Treat workers fairly and consistently. When a supervisor regularly praises the performance of one worker over others who perform equally well, he or she is showing favoritism. A supervisor who bends company policies for some workers is also showing favoritism. This type of preferential treatment has a demotivating effect on the other workers but may also put you and your company at risk for legal penalties.

Delegating Improperly

If you don't give an employee the authority necessary to accomplish a delegated task, you set the employee up for failure from the outset. Giving authority doesn't necessarily mean turning a task completely over to an employee, no questions asked. As the manager, you must decide what level of authority the employee has—and clearly communicate it.

Just as disastrous as not providing an appropriate amount of authority is delegating a task to someone who's incapable of completing it no matter how much authority is granted. The reasons for this inability may range from lack of skills or knowledge to an already full work schedule to any one of a variety of obstacles.

In either instance—delegating without giving authority or delegating to the wrong person—the result is the same. The employee fails to successfully accomplish the goal, which leads to frustration and demotivation.

Communicating Poorly

When you don't communicate with employees, they won't know what's expected of them, and you won't know what kinds of challenges they face as they perform their jobs. In such a close-lipped environment, assumptions lead to misunderstandings, lack of production, and low morale.

Here are some keys to becoming an effective communicator:

- Make sure your message is clear.

- Practice active listening.

- Acknowledge the viewpoints of others, even if you don't agree.

- Use specific language, especially when giving instructions and setting deadlines.

- Make sure your language is free of bias.

- Repeat the messages of others to make sure you understand what is being said.

- Ask questions. If you're the speaker, ask questions to make sure your message has been understood. If you're the listener, ask questions to clarify points you're uncertain about.

- Make sure your body language is congruent, which means delivering the same message as your words.

Failing to Support and Train Employees

Workers bring both strengths and limitations to their jobs. A good manager recognizes that both must be addressed if workers are to grow professionally. Training obviously should focus on helping workers develop skills in areas where they are weak. Often, however, organizations overlook training in areas where workers may already be perceived as performing satisfactorily. It's important to provide workers with ongoing opportunities to keep their skills polished in these areas and to stay current with new developments. Remember, when the workers you manage are fully trained and capable of carrying out their job tasks, you and your organization are more likely to achieve your goals as well. Everybody wins—even the customer, who benefits from high-quality products or services.

Still, the number of men and women attending skill-building training programs who have been on the job for years, slugging it out, trying to do their best without an ounce of training is absolutely amazing. Give your employees the training they need to perform their jobs at a peak level of performance. If your company doesn't have a formal training program, look into outside specialists who can provide niche training. Or hold your own informal training sessions or schedule time every week for peer-to-peer training. Lunchtime video training sessions are yet another possibility.

The point is this: Identify the areas where employees can improve performance and develop professionally. Then schedule the training—pronto. Waiting for the right time, or for the money is a cop-out. Budget it, schedule it, get it done. You've probably heard this before—you're only as strong as the weakest link on your team.

Exhibiting "Wishy-Washy" Behavior

Employees want their leaders to be decisive, to take the lead, *to call the shots*. No doubt, making decisions means taking responsibility and "sticking your neck out." But if you lack self-confidence to do so, it's likely that the employees you manage will follow your lead. They will avoid making decisions as long as possible or refuse to make decisions altogether. When no one takes responsibility for decision making, work comes to a halt as a bottleneck is created at the point where the decision needs to be made.

Sometimes in these cases, employees will go ahead and make their own decisions to get around the bottleneck. The problem here is you may have various employees implementing several different solutions that may be at odds with each other or that may overlap, driving up project costs or contributing to delays.

"Take time to deliberate, but when the time for action arrives, stop thinking and go in."

—Andrew Jackson

When you're called upon to make a decision, gather all the relevant information. Good managers will seek the input of others if the situation allows. This input can come from workers or fellow managers. (Remember from Chapter 2 that asking for suggestions from workers builds motivation.) Once you've gathered a number of alternatives, take time to discuss them and test them if time permits. Finally, make your decision and stick to it. Once you've implemented an alternative, continuously ask for feedback to find out areas where improvements are possible.

You cannot afford, practically speaking, to vacillate in making decisions or avoid making decisions. Doing so will negatively impact your ability to meet the demands of your job. More important, the level of respect workers have for you will markedly decrease and influence other areas of the manager-worker relationship.

Failing to Emphasize Teamwork

Even if workers don't operate in a formal team situation, they are part of a larger group—a department, a work unit, the organization as a whole. Managers who don't encourage workers to come together periodically to share ideas, measure progress, and see how their individual job responsibilities fit into the larger picture risk creating an atmosphere in which employees work for their own goals, for their own gain, whether or not it's in the best interest of the organization. In fact, some managers go so far as to create an environment in which they actually pit their workers against those in other departments. The long-term result is hostility and animosity among workers. As a manager, concentrate on ways to bring workers together to achieve the overall team or organization goal.

Giving Employees the Impression That You're Concerned Only About Yourself

To let your own self-interest become the overriding reason for doing what you do will be noticed, with great disdain. Workers will challenge your motives if they believe you look out only for yourself. They may even begin to regard positive feedback and recognition as attempts to manipulate them. And you'll find yourself short on support and cooperation when you may need it most. It is important, therefore, to convey the mutual benefits of any project or workplace situation, particularly those involving change.

Displaying Poor Personal Work Habits

As a manager, you set an example for those you manage. If your own work area is in constant disarray, if you often put off completing tasks, if you don't value punctuality, or if you don't manage your time well, employees *will* notice. Not only will some of them get the message that what you're practicing is acceptable behavior, they won't respect you if you reprimand them for the same actions. Insisting on one standard for employees but having a different standard for yourself is a quick way to demotivate employees.

Tolerating Poor Performance

Nip poor performance in the bud immediately. It's contagious for one thing. If workers see that you tolerate certain behaviors in one person, they may start practicing those same behaviors themselves. Further, if you allow one worker to get away with actions that prohibit others from performing their jobs, you'll breed resentment—against the poorly performing worker and against yourself.

If in spite of your best efforts to motivate workers, one repeatedly exhibits unacceptable behavior or doesn't perform up to standards, take these steps:

- Observe and record, in specific language, what the unacceptable behavior is.

- Call a meeting to discuss your observations.

- Get to the point of the meeting right away.

- Don't apologize for having to call the meeting.

- Specifically state the behavior you've observed and when, without being emotional or combative. Direct the comments to the behavior, not to the person. Don't say, "You're always late and you look like a slob when you arrive." Rather, state how many times the person's been tardy and on what dates.

- Work with the employee to establish an improvement plan that specifically states what behavior is to be improved and by when.

Oversupervising

Also known as micromanaging, oversupervising involves managing every detail of a task you've assigned. When you oversupervise, the signal you send to employees is that you don't trust them and have confidence in their ability to successfully carry out their job responsibilities. Obviously, it's important to clearly communicate what must be done and by when, and to be available when employees need direction, but to look over their shoulders and nit-pick every step of the way stifles their desire to work.

Imposing Impossible Workloads

There's only so much time in a workday and only so many resources for getting things done. Still, you can't expect workers to spend night after night and every weekend working overtime. Worse, you can't expect workers to accomplish in an average workday what really requires overtime. Setting unreasonable quotas or impossible workloads is demoralizing. Employees never feel as if they've achieved their goals. They become frustrated and burn out. Turnover increases and production actually decreases.

54

Focusing Only on Negatives

Certainly poor performance and procedures that could be improved are areas that must be addressed. Those kinds of issues aren't the focus here. What is referred to here is an attitude—one that sees more of what's wrong with any situation than with what went right. As a manager with a negative attitude, you influence not only workers, but also upper management and customers. In fact, it's been noted that one person with a negative attitude can infect up to three hundred people. As a manager, learn to recognize a job that's well done. Credit the workers responsible and encourage them to celebrate that success.

"There are no hopeless situations; there are only men who have grown hopeless about them."

—Clare Boothe Luce

Motivation Checkup

Are your own actions contributing to a poor motivational climate in your organization? Place a check mark in the appropriate column to quickly rate the degree to which you practice these de-motivating behaviors and actions. Be honest.

Demorivnib

	Almost always	Sometimes	Rarely
1. Criticize workers in front of others	☐	☐	☑
2. Am dishonest	☐	☐	☑
3. Take credit for employees' work	☐	☐	☑
4. Am inaccessible	☐	☑	☐
5. Show favoritism	☐	☐	☑
6. Delegate improperly	☐	☑	☐
7. Communicate poorly	☐	☐	☑
8. Fail to support and train employees	☐	☑	☑
9. Exhibit "wishy-washy" behavior	☐	☑	☐
10. Fail to emphasize teamwork	☐	☐	☑

11. Show concern only
    for yourself ☐ ☐ ☑

12. Display poor personal
    work habits ☐ ☐ ☑

13. Tolerate poor performance ☐ ☐ ☑

14. Oversupervise ☐ ☑ ☐

15. Impose impossible
    workloads ☐ ☐ ☑

16. Focus on the negatives ☐ ☐ ☑

Did you recognize any of these behaviors in yourself? Choose
one or two that you marked "Almost always" and include a plan
for overcoming them in the overall Motivation Action Plan you
develop in the next chapter.

Chapter Four

A Motivation Action Plan

As a manager, *you* have the awesome responsibility of creating a work environment where motivation propels employees to success. Are you paving the way?

Dr. Douglas McGregor emphasizes this point: "The motivation, the potential for development, the capacity for assuming responsibility are all present in people. It is the responsibility of management to make it possible for people to recognize and develop these human characteristics for themselves."

Developing an Action Plan

What do you plan to do? The best approach to bringing the ideas in this book into reality is to actually create a written motivation action plan.

1. ***Choose the idea in this book that is most suitable for your supervisory situation.*** Remember to consider its fit with the overall organizational mission, your team or department goals, and compatibility with the individual workers you supervise.

2. ***Determine the specific steps you will need to take.*** What actions will you need to take—and in what order? Will you need approval or assistance? What will change as a result of the implementation? Who will be affected?

3. ***Write a goal statement for implementing the idea.*** The goal should have the following characteristics:

   - Written

   - Have a deadline

   - Specific (state exactly what will be accomplished)

   - Measurable (have some mechanism for assessing whether the goal was met)

4. ***Ask yourself each day, what am I doing today to achieve this goal?***

5. ***Once you have been successful with one suggestion, continue to review this book to continually add fresh approaches.*** Then write a new goal.

Motivation Action Plan

1. Write the idea:

_____

_____

_____

_____

_____

2. Write a goal statement:

_____

_____

_____

_____

_____

3. Develop the steps necessary for achieving the goal.

_____

_____

_____

_____

_____

Remember to check each day to make sure you're working to achieve the goal.

Dealing With Change

Yes, change. the very fact that you have created a motivation action plan indicates that you intend to introduce a change, something different, into the work environment. Although you intend for the change to result in a positive outcome, change is often viewed as negative. For your plan to be accepted, you must anticipate and overcome any negativity, anxiety, and/or resistance.

First, it's important to remember this simple but effective formula:

$$more = less$$

More employee participation equals less resistance to the change. You'll see this formula at work in each of the suggestions that follows:

Suggestion 1: Empower employees to become part of the change. There are several reasons people resist change, one of which is fear. Many people play "Gee, what if" scenarios over and over when a new idea is proposed. When you begin to implement your plan of action, it's essential that you invite those around you to identify how the change will influence them, benefit them, and improve their present situation.

"The fearful unbelief is unbelief in yourself."

—Thomas Carlyle

Suggestion 2: Keep employees informed. Communicate as much as you know about what is happening as a result of the change. One of the major reasons people resist change is fear of the unknown. If you communicate with employees and keep them informed, you put this fear to rest.

Suggestion 3: Break the change down into digestible chunks. If it makes it easier for employees, introduce the change gradually. You can give employees encouragement and help them focus on small steps they can take to move toward the future. Celebrate their small successes.

Suggestion 4: Answer the "What's in It For Me?" question. This suggestion is similar to Suggestion 1. Generally people will accept change when they see a personal benefit. Employees who are involved in determining the benefits of change are less likely to resist it. Assist employees in identifying what the change will do for them.

Suggestion 5: Give employees some control over the change. As employees begin to focus on the benefits of the desired change, provide them with the opportunity to control the steps to the change. Participants in change workshops have revealed that having control reduces the anxiety and stress associated with change implementation and increases their motivation to make the change.

People don't change their behavior unless it makes a difference for them to do so."

—Fran Tarkenton in *How to Motivate People: Team Strategy for Success*

Suggestion 6: Help employees assimilate the change. Once employees begin to experience change, help them assimilate it by reinforcing the personal benefits they're gaining.

As employees begin to demonstrate a willingness to assimilate change into their daily routine, they develop a commitment to the change, a willingness to stick to the plan of action. The change actually becomes integrated into the work environment, and employees begin to feel a sense of satisfaction in accomplishment. They readily see the payoffs associated with the change. They enjoy, and may even take credit for, their participation in the process. Employees can view their efforts to bring about change with personal respect and pride. The change becomes a part of their routine, and any lingering concerns vanish.

Chapter Five

A Personal Motivation Check-Up

"The best way to inspire people to superior performance is to convince them by everything you do and by your everyday attitude that you are wholeheartedly supporting them."

—Harold Geneen

Is there a relationship between your own level of motivation and the motivational level of those around you?

Quite simply, yes. Your attitudes, behaviors, and actions have influenced, are influencing, and will continue to influence everyone you come in contact with.

When you look around at those you supervise, you will actually see a reflection of your own behavior, actions, and attitude. It's as if you held a mirror up to your employees and saw your own reflection. If you don't like what you see when you hold up that figurative mirror, it's time for some fine-tuning of your own attitude. The techniques presented in this chapter will help you make the attitude adjustment needed to motivate *yourself* to develop and carry out a plan for creating a work climate in which motivated workers flourish.

Develop Personal Expectations

Seeing yourself in the role of creating, building, and maintaining a positive motivational work environment is the first step to your ultimate success. In other words, you have to *decide* to do it and then develop personal expectations. You can think of these expectations as your *goals,* specifically the goals you listed in your action plan. If you don't have any goals, you won't have anything to work toward, to be motivated to accomplish. Remember, Maslow's highest level of need is self-actualization, and Herzberg listed accomplishment as a "satisfier."

"Example is not the main thing in influencing others, it is the only thing."

—Albert Schweitzer, humanitarian

Positive Self-Talk

After setting your goals, practice positive self-talk to propel you towards success. Sometimes called *affirmations,* positive self-talk consists of positive, results-oriented sentences that you repeat to yourself, over and over in the first person. Here are some examples relating to your goal to provide an environment in which workers can be motivated:

"I have the desire and dedication to bring about positive change and to build a culture where motivation thrives."

"I have an action plan that will fulfill this desire."

"I have the courage and confidence to initiate the action plan."

Visualization and Self-Talk

One of the most powerful, effective, and simple ways to increase your confidence, boost your self-esteem, and accomplish your goal is to practice visualization. Picture your desired outcome. See yourself making the changes necessary to achieving your goal, enlisting the support of others, and reaping the rewards of an environment in which you and your workers are motivated.

Keep this picture in your mind. Then ask yourself how much of what you picture you're currently doing.

Combining visualization and self-talk will rapidly help you to get in touch with your own sense of commitment and how you plan to bring about positive outcomes.

One way to activate your potential for visualization and positive self-talk is to practice deep relaxation techniques. Research indicates that when you are in a deeply relaxed state of mind, you are more effective in communicating positive messages through your self-talk. You can navigate purposely towards positive outcomes.

When your inner speech and inner thoughts are in sync and focused on your goal, outwardly your nonverbal and verbal communication and your actions will match. Thus, your entire focus is movement towards goal achievement.

Here are the key steps to relaxing yourself so you can hear your positive inner voice and visualize yourself successfully achieving your goal:

1. ***Find a quiet place with no interruptions.*** Start by putting your mind in neutral. Close your eyes.

2. ***Breathe deeply.*** Begin by slowing your breathing patterns. Count from 1 to 10 slowly.

   (If you have a different relaxation technique you use successfully and would like to use instead, go right ahead. The point is to become deeply relaxed, not to worry about how to get there.)

3. ***Talk to your inner self.*** See yourself actually experiencing the desired results. Feel the emotion (joy, satisfaction, happiness, less stress, optimism) associated with achieving your goal. Spend three to four minutes fully involved in this positive state of mind.

Self-talk and visualization are amazing in their power. Top achievers in every industry, from sports to the military, have discovered that self-talk and visualization have helped them reap rich dividends.

When you are personally motivated toward creating a positive, productive, and motivated group of workers, your own enthusiasm will infect the workers you supervise.

Although you can't personally motivate another person, you *can* influence, persuade, and become a role model to others, which no doubt will have a significant impact on their level of motivation and their behaviors. How you behave in day-to-day situations, even difficult ones, and the outcomes that result from your actions will be quickly sized up by others. Mark Twain aptly said, "Few things are harder to put up with than the annoyance of a good example." Are you that good example?

Bibliography and Suggested Reading

Alessandra, Tony. *Communicating at Work*. New York: Simon & Schuster, 1993.

Blanchard, Kenneth, Patricia Zigarmi, and Drea Zigarmi. *Leadership and the One Minute Manager*. New York: William Morrow, 1985.

Brown, Jerry, and Denise Dudley. *The Supervisor's Guide*. Mission, KS: SkillPath Publications, 1989.

Daniels, Aubrey C. *Bringing Out the Best in People*. New York: McGraw-Hill, 1994.

70

Herzberg, Frederick, et al. *The Motivation to Work*. New York: Wiley, 1959.

Jandt, Fred E. *Straight Answers to People Problems*. New York: Irwin, 1994.

Maslow, Abraham H. *Motivation and Personality*. New York: Harper & Row, 1954.

McGregor, Douglas. *The Human Side of Enterprise*. New York: McGraw-Hill, 1960.

Miskell, Jane R., and Vincent Miskell. *Motivation at Work*. New York: Business One Irwin, 1994.

Poley, Michelle Fairfield. *A Winning Attitude*. Mission, KS: SkillPath Publications, 1992.

Scott, Gini Graham. *The Empowered Mind*. Englewood Cliffs, NJ: Prentice Hall, 1994.

Towers, Mark. *The ABC's of Empowered Teams*. Mission, KS: SkillPath Publications, 1994.

Towers, Mark. *Dynamic Delegation!* Mission, KS: SkillPath Publications, 1994.

Available From SkillPath Publications

Self-Study Sourcebooks

Climbing the Corporate Ladder: What You Need to Know and Do to Be a Promotable Person *by Barbara Pachter and Marjorie Brody*

Coping With Supervisory Nightmares: 12 Common Nightmares of Leadership and What You Can Do About Them *by Michael and Deborah Singer Dobson*

Defeating Procrastination: 52 Fail-Safe Tips for Keeping Time on Your Side *by Marlene Caroselli, Ed.D.*

Discovering Your Purpose *by Ivy Haley*

Going for the Gold: Winning the Gold Medal for Financial Independence *by Lesley D. Bissett, CFP*

Having Something to Say When You Have to Say Something: The Art of Organizing Your Presentation *by Randy Horn*

Info-Flood: How to Swim in a Sea of Information Without Going Under *by Marlene Caroselli, Ed.D.*

The Innovative Secretary *by Marlene Caroselli, Ed.D.*

Mastering the Art of Communication: Your Keys to Developing a More Effective Personal Style *by Michelle Fairfield Poley*

Obstacle Illusions: Coverting Crisis to Opportunity *by Marlene Caroselli, Ed.D.*

Organized for Success! 95 Tips for Taking Control of Your Time, Your Space, and Your Life *by Nanci McGraw*

A Passion to Lead! How to Develop Your Natural Leadership Ability *by Michael Plumstead*

P.E.R.S.U.A.D.E.: Communication Strategies That Move People to Action *by Marlene Caroselli, Ed.D.*

Productivity Power: 250 Great Ideas for Being More Productive *by Jim Temme*

Promoting Yourself: 50 Ways to Increase Your Prestige, Power, and Paycheck *by Marlene Caroselli, Ed.D.*

Proof Positive: How to Find Errors Before They Embarrass You *by Karen L. Anderson*

Risk-Taking: 50 Ways to Turn Risks Into Rewards *by Marlene Caroselli, Ed.D. and David Harris*

Stress Control: How You Can Find Relief From Life's Daily Stress *by Steve Bell*

The Technical Writer's Guide *by Robert McGraw*

Total Quality Customer Service: How to Make It Your Way of Life *by Jim Temme*

Write It Right! A Guide for Clear and Correct Writing *by Richard Andersen and Helene Hinis*

Your Total Communication Image *by Janet Signe Olson, Ph.D.*

Handbooks

The ABC's of Empowered Teams: Building Blocks for Success *by Mark Towers*

Assert Yourself! Developing Power-Packed Communication Skills to Make Your Points Clearly, Confidently, and Persuasively *by Lisa Contini*

Breaking the Ice: How to Improve Your On-the-Spot Communication Skills
by Deborah Shouse

The Care and Keeping of Customers: A Treasury of Facts, Tips, and Proven Techniques for Keeping Your Customers Coming BACK! *by Roy Lantz*

Challenging Change: Five Steps for Dealing With Change *by Holly DeForest and Mary Steinberg*

Dynamic Delegation: A Manager's Guide for Active Empowerment *by Mark Towers*

Every Woman's Guide to Career Success *by Denise M. Dudley*

Grammar? No Problem! *by Dave Davies*

Great Openings and Closings: 28 Ways to Launch and Land Your Presentations With Punch, Power, and Pizazz *by Mari Pat Varga*

Hiring and Firing: What Every Manager Needs to Know *by Marlene Caroselli, Ed.D. with Laura Wyeth, Ms.Ed.*

How to Be a More Effective Group Communicator: Finding Your Role and Boosting Your Confidence in Group Situations *by Deborah Shouse*

How to Deal With Difficult People *by Paul Friedman*

Learning to Laugh at Work: The Power of Humor in the Workplace *by Robert McGraw*

Making Your Mark: How to Develop a Personal Marketing Plan for Becoming More Visible and More Appreciated at Work *by Deborah Shouse*

Meetings That Work *by Marlene Caroselli, Ed.D.*

The Mentoring Advantage: How to Help Your Career Soar to New Heights *by Pam Grout*

Minding Your Business Manners: Etiquette Tips for Presenting Yourself Professionally in Every Business Situation *by Marjorie Brody and Barbara Pachter*

Misspeller's Guide *by Joel and Ruth Schroeder*

Motivation in the Workplace: How to Motivate Workers to Peak Performance and Productivity *by Barbara Fielder*

NameTags Plus: Games You Can Play When People Don't Know What to Say *by Deborah Shouse*

Networking: How to Creatively Tap Your People Resources *by Colleen Clarke*

New & Improved! 25 Ways to Be More Creative and More Effective *by Pam Grout*

Power Write! A Practical Guide to Words That Work *by Helene Hinis*

The Power of Positivity: Eighty ways to energize your life *by Joel and Ruth Schroeder*

Putting Anger to Work For You *by Ruth and Joel Schroeder*

Reinventing Your Self: 28 Strategies for Coping With Change *by Mark Towers*

Saying "No" to Negativity: How to Manage Negativity in Yourself, Your Boss, and Your Co-Workers *by Zoie Kaye*

The Supervisor's Guide: The Everyday Guide to Coordinating People and Tasks *by Jerry Brown and Denise Dudley, Ph.D.*

Taking Charge: A Personal Guide to Managing Projects and Priorities *by Michal E. Feder*

Treasure Hunt: 10 Stepping Stones to a New and More Confident You! *by Pam Grout*

A Winning Attitude: How to Develop Your Most Important Asset! *by Michelle Fairfield Poley*

For more information, call 1-800-873-7545.